Horse Po

Compiled by John Foster

OXFORD

Oxford University Press, Walton Street, Oxford OX2 6DP

Oxford New York Toronto
Delhi Bombay Calcutta Madras Karachi
Petaling Jaya Singapore Hong Kong Tokyo
Nairobi Dar es Salaam Cape Town
Melbourne Auckland

and associated companies in
Berlin Ibadan

Oxford is a trade mark of Oxford University Press

© Oxford University Press 1991
Printed in Hong Kong

A CIP catalogue record for this book is available from the British
Library.

Acknowledgements
The Editor and Publisher wish to thank the following who have
kindly given permission for the use of copyright material:

John Foster for 'The Old Horse' and 'Magic Horse' both © 1990 John
Foster; Julie Holder for 'Watching horses and riders' © 1990 Julie
Holder; Jean Kenword for 'The Rider', 'The Great White Horse' and
'The Foal' all © 1990 Jean Kenward; John Kitching for 'The Old
Rocking Horse' and 'Horses' both © 1990 John Kitching; Judith
Nicholls for 'When?' © 1990 Judith Nicholls, included by permission
of the author; Jill Townsend for 'Zebras' © 1990 Jill Townsend.

Although every effort has been made to contact the owners of
copyright material, a few have been impossible to trace, but if they
contact the Publisher correct acknowledgement will be made in
future editions.

Magic horse

Black horse,
Magic horse,
Carry me away,
Over the river,
Across the bay
To the sandy beach
Where I can play.

Black horse,
Magic horse,
Carry me away,
Over the seas
To the forest trees
Where I can watch
The tiger cubs play.

2

Black horse,
Magic horse,
Carry me away
To Arctic snows
Where the cold wind blows,
Where I can watch
The polar bears play.

Black horse,
Magic horse,
Carry me away
To golden sands
In far-away lands
Where the sea is blue
And I can play all day.

John Foster

The Old Rocking Horse

The old rocking horse
Is now worn, with no tail
And no mane. His brown paint
Is all cracked. But the course
That he rides without fail
Day and night with his quaint,
Mended smile stays the same:
There's no end to his galloping game.

John Kitching

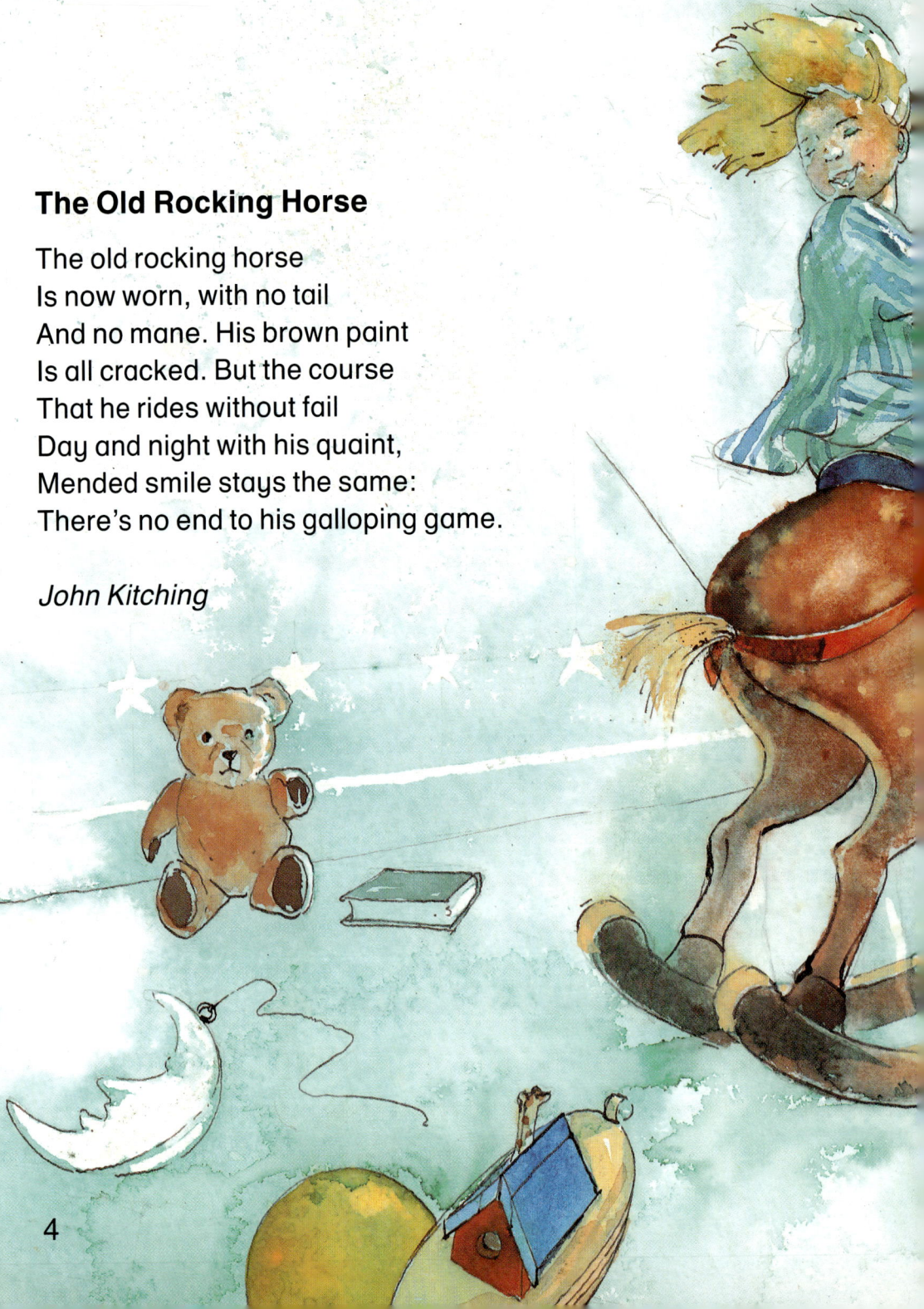

4

When?

Where will you take me, magic horse,
with your mane-like wings unfurled?
Will you take me high through the midnight sky?

We'll see the world!

How will you take me, magic horse,
do you ride on a magic track?
Your shoes are gold, so I've been told . . .

They'll bring us back!

When will you take me, magic horse,
with the clover on your brow?
When shall we race through starry space?

I'll take you now!

Judith Nicholls

Watching horses and riders

Look –
He rides like a knight on a milk-white charger,
And she's on a racehorse first past the post
And there is a horse that looks much larger,
Or is the rider smaller than most?

There is a rider coolly sucking a lolly,
And that one with a cornet digs in his toes
As up and over goes his horse,
Now he's got a blob of ice-cream on his nose.

Quick! Quick! Look at that –
There's an old lady
Riding that black horse
And wearing a cowboy hat!

Oh look – there's Nadine and Kerry,
Sailing by with a wave and a grin,
Just to watch them riding round so fast
Makes my head spin.

Oh, it's all over,
All of them winners
The riders climb down and up goes the shout –
'CAN WE HAVE ANOTHER GO?'
On the fairground roundabout.

Julie Holder

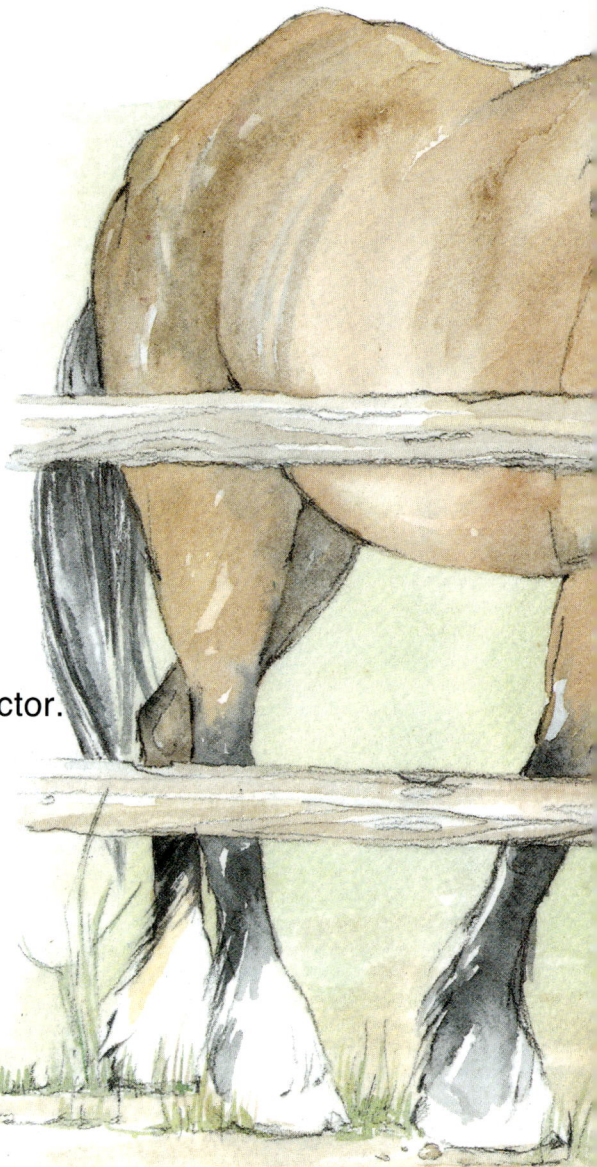

The Old Horse

When we go for a walk down the lane,
The old horse hears us coming.
So he comes to stand and wait
For us by the gate.

When we get out the bread
To feed him,
He bends his large head
And we reach up
To stroke his nose.

Then, off he goes
To graze
And dream again of the days
When he used to pull
The coalman's cart
And the farmer's plough.

Then, he was as strong as a tractor.
He is too old now
To work any longer,
But in the old days
There was no one stronger.

John Foster

The Rider

Rider, rider
in the Square,
where are you going?
Tell me where?

Your huge stone horse
is hard and grey:
one hoof is raised
to trot away.

His mane is flying
and his eye
is fixed upon
the windy sky. . . .

People stare,
and buses pass,
and children scamper
on the grass,

And yet you never
move a bit.
How many years
will you sit

Rider, silent
in the Square?
Where are you going?
Tell me, where?

Jean Kenward

The Great White Horse

Have you seen the Great White Horse
    great white horse,
      great white horse?
Have you seen the great white horse
    that's carved
      upon the hill?

Have you stroked his chalky mane,
    chalky mane,
      chalky mane?
Did you let him loose again
    or leave him
      lying still?

Did you see his waking eye,
   waking eye
      waking eye –
open to the windy sky
   by day and night
      until

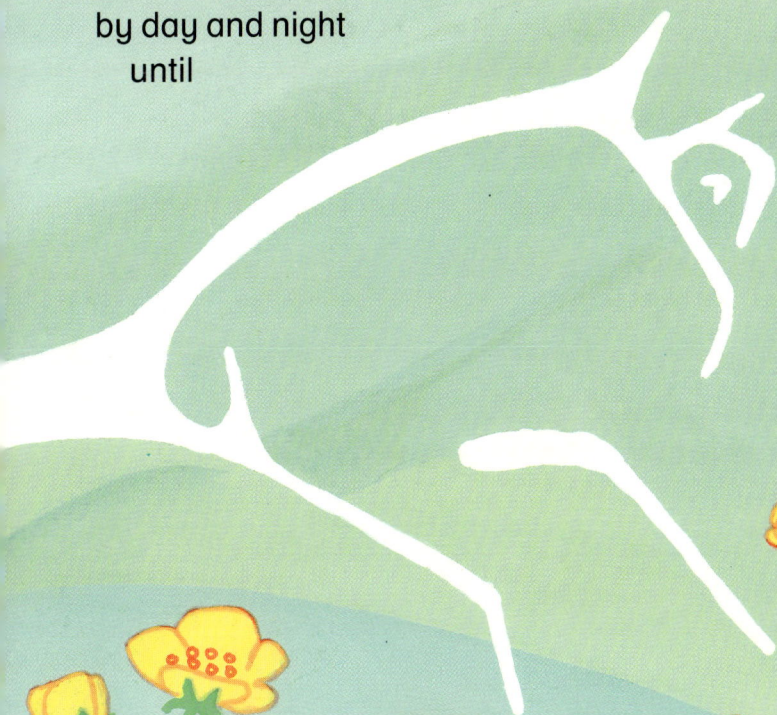

Buttercups grow over him
      over him
         over him:
rub him out from rim to rim
      the horse
         upon the hill!

Jean Kenward

13

The Foal

There's something new in the meadow:
it's soft, and brown and small
but its legs are long and straggly,
it can hardly stand at all.

The grey mare, gently breathing
there, in the lush, wet green,
has a new-born foal beside her
as limp as plasticine.

He rose, as we stopped to wonder,
and wobbled a little bit,
as if he were lately come to the world
and wasn't too sure of it.

Then he turned, and touched his mother,
searching her drowsed and dim
for the warm, sweet milk she carried.

What name shall we give to him?

Jean Kenward

Zebras

Zebras are
   horses in hiding,
shadowy
   in between strips of leaves,
watching
   for the sun-coloured
lion
   who is always hunting them.

Jill Townsend

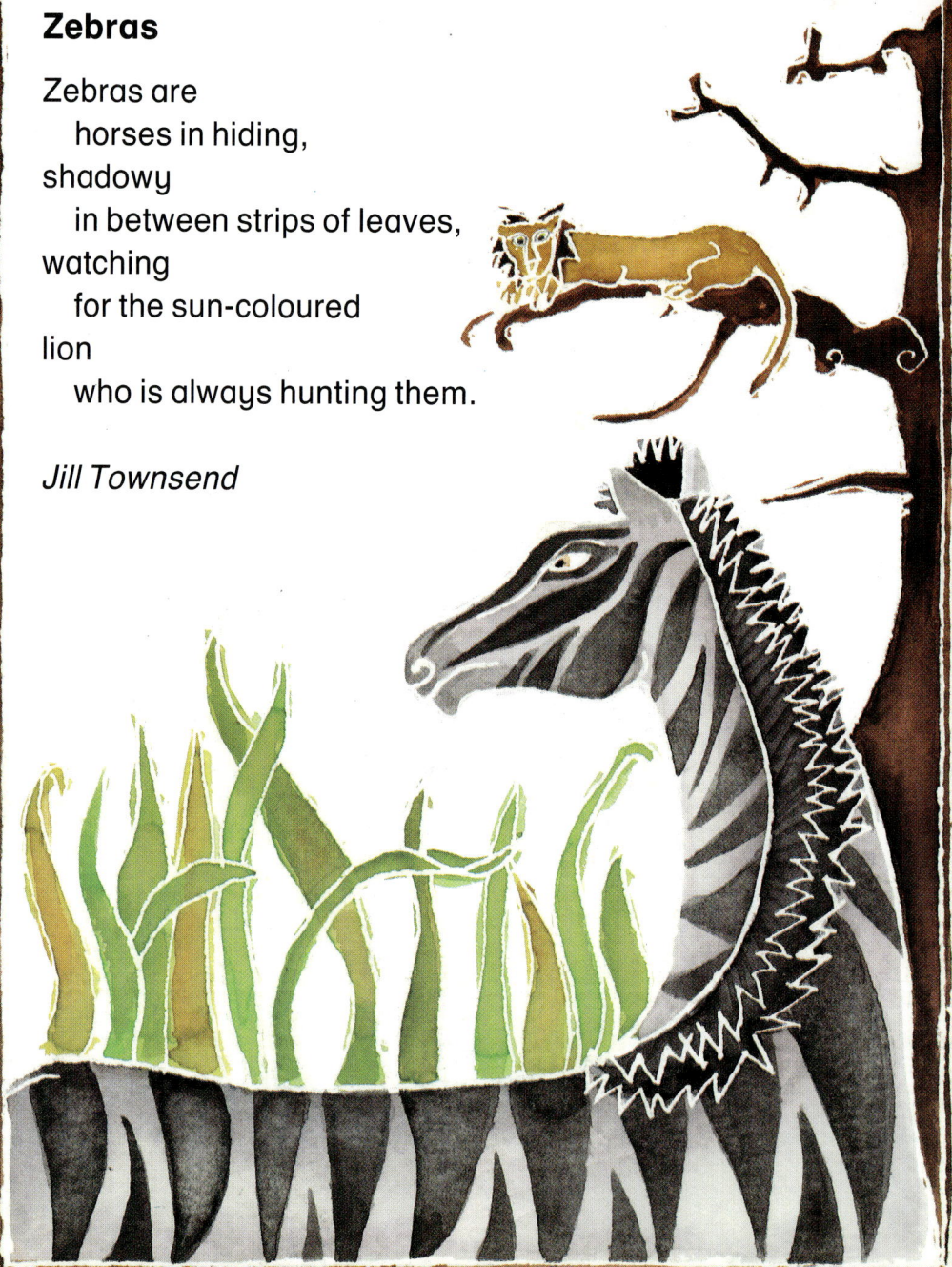